Hedge Hog

& SUPERCAT

written by:
Cadell Orion Hosten

Illustrated by:
Beon King

Author Reputation Press LLC
45 Dan Road Suite 36
Canton MA 02021
www.authorreputationpress.com
Hotline: 1(800) 220-7660
Fax: 1(855) 752-6001

Ordering Information:
Quantity Sales. Special discounts are available on quantity purchases by corporations, associations, and others. For details, contact the publisher at the address above.

Printed in the United States of America.

ISBN-13	Softcover	978-1-64961-285-4
	eBook	978-1-64961-286-1

Library of Congress Control Number: 2021906173

ACKNOWLEDGEMENT

I thank God, who is the author and finisher of my fate.

To my Grandmother:
Latifah El, thank you for all your love and support; you are always here for all of my needs. I have questions I need answers to when I need someone to talk to; you take me to the Park to play. Grandma, I could go on and on all day about how much I love you and all the reasons why so I will just say I THANK GOD FOR YOU BEING MY GRANDMOTHER!

To my parents:
Levar and Crystal Hosten, thank you for all of your love and support, thank you for loving me the way you do, and for always encouraging me to follow my dreams and to see them through. Thank you guys for Believing in me even when I didn't think I could get through this book; you guys made me I have the best Mom and dad thanks I LOVE Y'ALL.

Thank you to everyone who contributed in any way to ensure that this book went into the completion.

Krissy D., thank you for your encouraging words.

Dr. Lance, thank you for connecting me to such an awesome publishing company.

It's different Team
MS4RREAL aka mommy
The real Hawa cosmetics aka auntie Hawa
Brooklyn's finest
Dj Hercules
Thank you guys for your love and the gift of your Financial assistance.
You guys are great love y'all

And to the host of others thank you for your love
your encouragement and support.

Auntie Cheryl, LOVE YOU TO THE MOON AND BACK.
Thank you for all that you do.
Auntie Angie, I love you and thank you for all that you do.
Kareen, love you and thank you.
Auntie Vossie, Thank you for all you.
Uncle Lloyd and Uncle Jermaine,
thank you for always pushing me to be great.
Larenze London and Jeremiah, thank you for helping me
to learn to read and spell I will never forget it!
TYLAYA, THANK YOU BIG SISTER, I LOVE YOU!!!
Rocky and Uncle Kevin thank you for always pushing me to be great.

Aunt Sylvia a.k.a. my pickles thank you for loving me and encouraging me
the way you do love you
Uncle Bernard, I love you and thank you for all you do.
Lil Leonard You always keep me in line I love you.

I hope I didn't forget anyway but just in case I did I'm only seven years old
and I love you guys all thank you so much for your love and support,
as well as your words of encouragement.

Once upon a time, there was a young boy name,
Cadell. He was born in Nassau and came home
from the hospital to his home in South Jamaica,
Queens, N.Y. When Cadell turned 5 years of age,
his parents decided that they wanted to expose
him to a different life. So, they packed their
bags and moved to the Pocanos in Pennsylvania.

One day Cadell and his mom were riding on the highway heading to run some errands. Cadell looked to the right of him at the window and saw a deer laying down on the side of the road, dead. Cadell began to cry while saying, "Mom, pull over!!"

Cadell's mom, not sure what was taking place, quickly pulled to the side of the road. Cadell's mom asked what was wrong.

After a brief explanation, Cadell asked his mom if it would be okay for him to get out of the car and pray for the dead deer.

When Cadell stepped out of the car, he felt a sharp pain in his right arm. "Ouch!" he yelled.

Mom asked if he was okay and he replied, "I'm okay." He quickly approached the deer and started praying.

As he opened the door, out of the corner of his eye, he saw the deer start to shake. Cadell was surprised, "Mom! wait, I think I prayed the deer back to life" "What??? Let's look!" As Mom got out of the car and started walking around, the deer sprang to its feet and ran into the woods. Cadell was so excited he yelled, "Mom! what just happened? Did I do it? Did I do it? Did I do it?!"

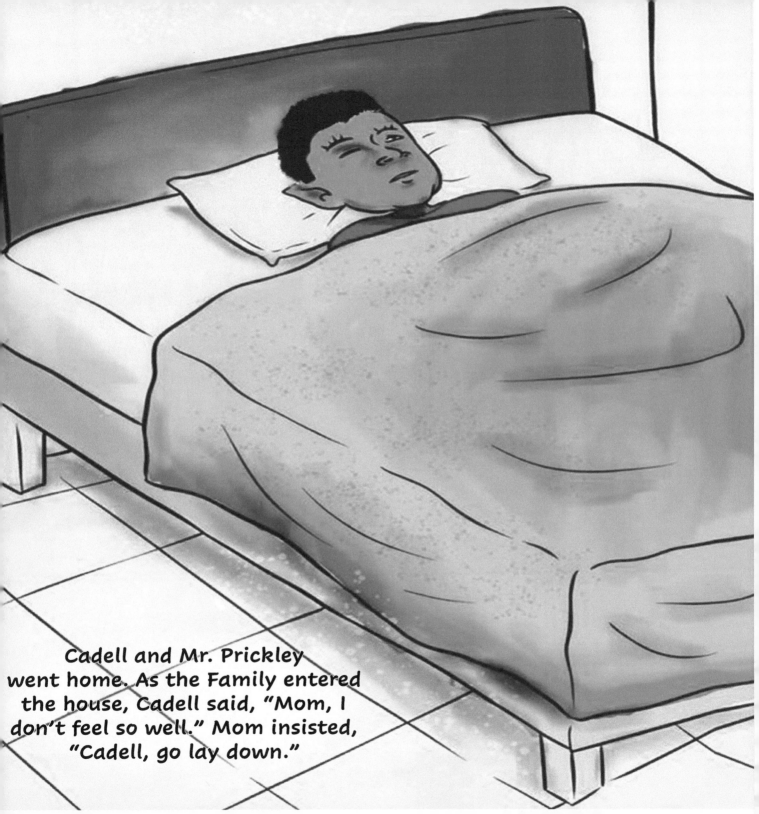

Cadell and Mr. Prickley went home. As the Family entered the house, Cadell said, "Mom, I don't feel so well." Mom insisted, "Cadell, go lay down."

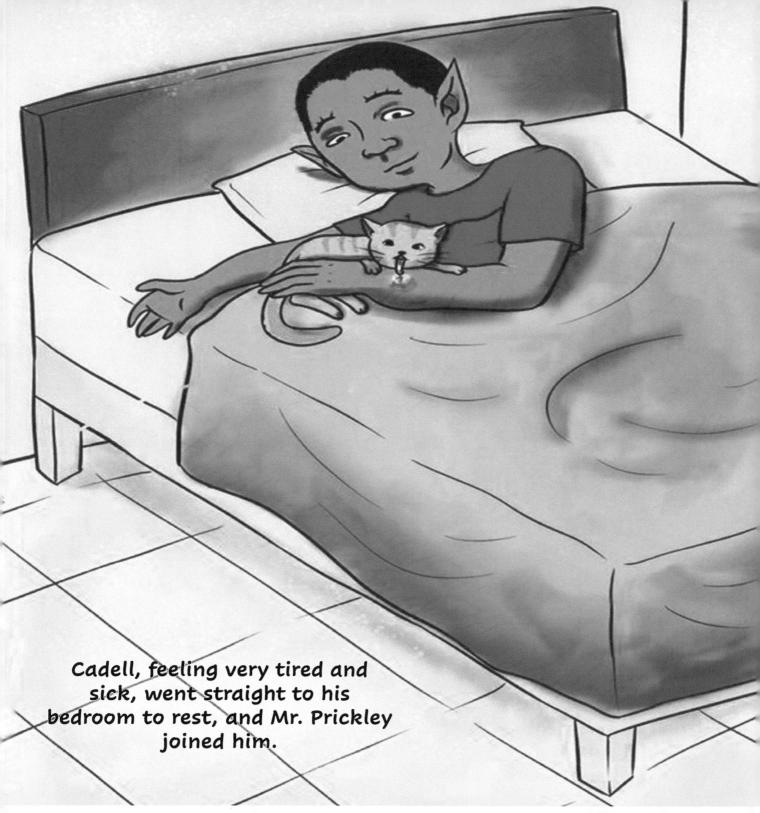

Cadell, feeling very tired and sick, went straight to his bedroom to rest, and Mr. Prickley joined him.

When Mom entered Cadell's bedroom, He said, "Mom, I'm really hot." Cadell's mom, Crystal, took a temperature and put a cold washcloth on his forehead to cool him off. She also gave Mr. Prickley a cool bath because he appeared to be a little sick too.

The following day, Cadell woke up feeling much better; he went into the bathroom to brush his teeth. When Cadell looked in the mirror, he yelled, "Aahh!" Cadell could not believe his eyes; he looked like a Hedgehog.

As Cadell stood in total disbelief, Mr. Prickley walked up to Cadell and Purred; however, it was different than any other time. Cadell and Mr. Prickley understood exactly what one another was saying.

It was at the moment, that Cadell understood exactly what had taken place. He and Mr. Prickley had been given the gift of healing and understanding animals.

Cadell talked it over with Mr. Prickley and decided they needed new names because of the gifts they had received.

CPSIA information can be obtained
at www.ICGtesting.com
Printed in the USA
LVHW072346010721
691745LV00001B/37